LIGHT LINES
*Three Line Thursday
Anthology*

LIGHT LINES
Three Line Thursday
Anthology

EDITED BY
GRACE BLACK

Light Lines: Three Line Thursday Anthology
Copyright © 2015 by Three Line Thursday
All rights reserved. No part of this book may be reproduced, scanned, or distributed in any printed or electronic form without prior written permission from the authors.

www.threelinethursday.com

This book is a work of fiction. Names, characters, places, and incidents either are products of the authors' imagination or are used fictitiously. Any resemblance to actual persons, living or dead, events, or locales is entirely coincidental.

Cover photo by Matt Adamik Photography

www.facebook.com/MattAdamikPhotography

DEDICATION

POETRY IS NOT DEAD

THREE LINE THURSDAY WINNERS

Year One

WHAT CAN YOU SAY
IN ONLY
THREE LINES—

BLOODY SNOWFLAKES ON A ROASTING TONGUE
DISSOLVING INTO A BLUSHING POOL OF YOU
LINGERING, REFUSING TO BE SWALLOWED

CHRIS MILAM

OUR CORRODED DALLIANCE
FORGED BY DECEITFUL ASSURANCES
MANACLING MY ESSENCE TO YOUR WILL

IMAGE RONIN

Yes, you may leave me
But your words, they still linger
In the air I breathe

Nan Holmes

The path was laid in cold iron
Straight and sturdily south
It seemed only, I saw it pointed north

                                    Matt Milano

A PLAINTIVE PLEA;
YOUR ICY RESPONSE
BURNING TO THE TOUCH

GEOFF HOLME

THE GIANT'S TEARS BLUR HIS VISION
THE SIMPLEST OF ACTS CAN TOUCH US MOST
THEY'D RAISED THE BRIDGE ROOF BY 3 FEET

DAVID SHAKES

> Look down to the gutter and you will find me
> Bent and distorted, but somehow
> Still straining for the sky

Karl A. Russell

Forgotten alongside an abandoned road,
The old tire. Missing its hub and road-worn,
Yet its moss grows young and green with promise

KT Phillips

I HAD THOUGHT SPECTERS TO BE WHISPERS IN THE DARK, FAINT ECHOES OF FORMS, BUT HERE I AM—ALONE—STARING AT THE LAST THING YOUR FEET TOUCHED, HAUNTED BY A CHAIR

CASEY ROSE FRANK

The birds have flown
Too cold to stay
Next year, I'll knit them sweaters

Matt Lashley

"I can swallow the sea," you crowed, so we dared the reef
It coughed me up but caught you in its barnacled gullet
The tide rushes in, testing your claim

Nancy Chenier

It's divided: the canyon, your heart
Paths unfinished, precarious panels
But you cross it, traverse the depths to the next stop

Brian Puglisi

Makeshift camp by a pristine stream
I gathered tinder; you'd forgotten the matches
We were hungry that night, but not cold

David Borrowdale

His outline is familiar, through her drunken eyes. The ghostly hand reaching, offering her the comfort she seeks with one last drink, she takes it, leaving the fabric behind

Mira Day

I AWOKE AND FOUND A WORLD FOLDED IN TWO;
AN INK BLOT TEST DECIDING OUR FUTURE
I SAW ADVENTURE, YOU SAW DISASTER

CASEY ROSE FRANK

Running—we wash the night's revelries & indiscretions
From new-born Saturday's electric tears, we emerge clean
Collecting moments, reincarnated as thinly veiled stories

Rose Ketring

If I had Crayolas, I'd draw a picture
Of a bird, a fence, using all the wrong colors
But they'd still be right—to me

Michael Seese

Rows of carved stones honor the lost
Yet only I
Mourn the artist

Lauren Akers Chiles

TIME COUGHED, HUMORLESS, FIXATED MINUTIA
RADIATING ITS POISON DOWN UPON US,
RUSTED BONES, RUSTED MINDS, FRESH COFFINS

Brett Milam

You failed to illustrate more than my curves & edges
Primary color adjectives when you should have been able to
capture the fabric of my soul

                                                    Casey Rose Frank

Douse me in your gasoline
Fingertips like matches
Light me up, till nothing's left but ashes

Nan Holmes

Nature's lush textures thicken and weave the bower, providing shelter from predator, offering concealment from prey, I linger there a moment; the vicious cycle paused

Elaine Marie McKay

I BEND TO THE SHAPE OF THIS TUMULTUOUS LOVE
BOWED IN A CRESCENT'S CURVE, BEFORE BEING FLUNG
AND LEFT AS FLOTSAM TO DRIFT IN SEA-SALT STING

ELAINE MARIE MCKAY

The lady jumped from the third story window
She tried to fly, but she was better at falling,
So she did that—

CARLOS OROZCO

He was an artist of patinas
But the more he painted over the past,
The more she kept bleeding through

Voima Oy

One tank of gas
One stolen car key
There lies freedom

Michael Seese

As I grew older, I learned to love
Stark beauty—the loneliness in nature
Somehow, it rounds out my hollow places

Emily Livingstone

Your small fingers grip the pencil
With the same insecure force that you
Squeeze my hand, coloring both in shades of memory

Tamara Shoemaker

Our legs swing, moldy plastic pinching exposed skin
Ashy nubs and leftover happy juice our plunder,
We're adults until mom finds out

Foy S. Iver

We sat on the edge of the universe
Demigods lost in a daring plight
To gather galaxies in our trembling hands

Hannah Fields

Lifted hands from clocks, love me, love-me-nots, feather-
weight keepsakes, a ruffled skirt scatters breezeways
Starbursts swallow the sun; darling, you've left me undone

Sherry Sutton Curtiss

Crows gathering in rebel clouds for a fly-past
Then wings into heart and soul for a singing lark
Putting another bullet in the gun for you

PAUL JOHN WELSH

The guilt that paints a liar's tongue
Soon cracks and peels
And with that, comes revelation

Stephanie Ellis

It was here, on this still water, where you decided
To leave the cradles of this boat and your life
And thus, disturb to rippling chaos the waters of mine

David W. Blackstone

Mellow-yellow clouds and shoe laced power lines
Bare feet keep Papa's whiskey secrets
If I were you, I'd use those wings

Foy S. Iver

Vacant eyes, an internal house-riot
Those endless nights on a worn-out sofa
Mumbling obscenities & Never-Nots

Nan Holmes

The raspberry jam you jarred, wood smoke in your hair,
Lavender soap neck curves and caramel blackberry kisses
I've distilled your scents; a single drop of memory

Casey Rose Frank

I LET THE SEA IN
MEASURE THE WEIGHT OF THE CHILD LOST TO OUR ARMS
AS YOUR COASTLINE WITHDRAWS INTO SILENCE

DAZMB

Here, a single breath and we travel back in time
A hidden pocket of scent, wet fallen leaves, wood smoke
Though our shirts still carry dry scent of summer sun

Casey Rose Frank

In broken bowls and abandoned cups, we mixed potions bright and tart as forlorn fruit. Summer-stained fingers, the only proof of our transgressions

Foy S. Iver

The subdued light of your fractured psyche sways
Quivers down the wick of its existence
Shuddering as it reaches an inevitable extinguishment

Jennifer Todhunter

But with a single brushstroke
Reality will glaze every rainbow harsh-brown
and scrub all the sunsets dry

Jacki Donnellan

The shell echoed with the lost memories
Carousels and candy floss
And now the tracks of salty tears

Christine Holden

They stretch as the eye sees, switching kaleidoscopic;
The spectres of choices contemplated
Never weres made never ares, beyond our grasping reach

Catherine Connolly

Three Line Thursday Artists
Year One

A PICTURE'S WORTH
A THOUSAND WORDS
YOU GET THIRTY

Photo by Gidget Bates

The chains hold back the ghosts
But the ghosts own her heart
And she finds them in every shot

                                        Gidget Bates

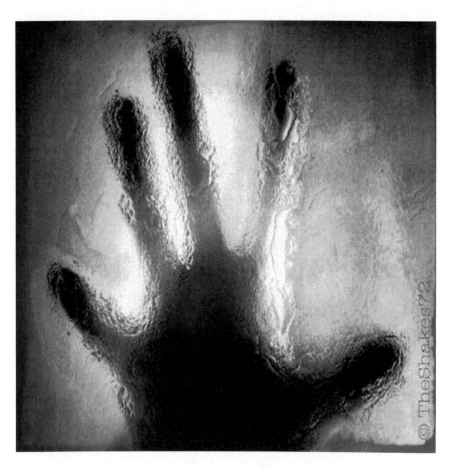

Photo by David Shakes

Frosted bathroom glass doubles as a membrane
Pushing against the limits of their boundaries, surface
Tension breaks, flooding eternity with liquid darkness

                                        David Shakes

PHOTO BY TRACY ANN

THE TWIG:
WHEN YOU CHANGE YOUR PERSPECTIVE
YOU WILL SEE—EVERYTHING HAS BEAUTY

TRACY ANN

PHOTO BY BORIS BODEN

Human Powered, Pedal Driven
Stopping to rest
It still remains

                              Boris Boden

Photo by Matt Adamik

The fire inside me
I'd feed it to you freely
If you'd swallow it whole

Matt Adamik

Art by F. E. Clark

Title: "Keep an Eye Out for Signs," she said.
Inspired by a mentor's advice on finding one's own path
Texture & colour from the Scottish skies, seas, & landscape

F. E. Clark

Photo by Bev Flynn

My structured soul explodes in want & wanderlust
I'm stability, the knowing now, couldn't leave. Restlessness
below my skin bares cosmic rust. Still—I dream

Bev Flynn

Photo by Karin Taylor

Upon seeing this dandelion, I found myself drawn to it. Photographing it with my iPhone, felt like I'd given it a little thank you kiss for just being there—

KARIN TAYLOR

Photo by Adriana Hawks

Awakening skies beckon
To fly toward silver linings
I chose to turn away

ADRIANA HAWKS

PHOTO BY LISA SHAMBROOK

We have need of nothing more from earth's entangled hand
Than tears from heaven, fire from dust and cobweb breath
Bequeathed from starlight threaded strand

Lisa Shambrook

Photo by Soulhearts

Not the you nor I, but the you and I
It's the we in us that fuels the fire
Bright, shining flames untouched by shame

                              Soulhearts

Special Challenge Winners
Year One

It's not what
others see
It's what you feel

Rank and file of stone
Names, dates, and foreign places
Enjoy your freedom

David Borrowdale

Corroded conscience
Rejuvenates with the oil
Of your tender words

David Borrowdale

Shamed shadow, bereft
Bowed head, black thoughts whirl
At our mutual betrayal

Stephanie Ellis

Supine in darkness
I'll swallow my suffering,
For heat sharpens iron

DeRicki Johnson

VERDANT BOWER, LITHE
AS THE BACKS BENEATH IT,
A HEADY SHADE FOR RECKLESS HEARTS

AUGUSTA DORMAN

I STAND ON THE JETTY, AWAITING THE FERRYMAN
THE SUN SETS ON THE DAY, ON MY LIFE
HELL ISN'T OTHER PEOPLE...IT'S THE ETERNITY OF REGRET

DAVE JAMES ASHTON

Liquid verse, it swirls, within my soul of stone. Passion scrapes to seek escape, it's etched against my bones. Day of Reckoning, my words revealed, in strands of color

Bev Flynn

She's clutching firmly to her darkness, where's she's been
For so long—letting go is unfamiliar, unknown—
Without darkness, there might be nothing left

Emily Livingstone

Sycamores endure. Spalted masonry bursts the veneer of paint. Across the street, crimes of voluntary ignorance accumulate. Closed blinds mask, the lost & lonely who wait

F. E. Clark

But one day I'll have a home with a garden
Nodding roses, close-cut grass, and jasmine climbing
Up my headstone—

                                                    Jacki Donnellan

Unwashed windows watch the world—witnessing wickedness they watched you walk away from your wrongdoing. The dirt whispered as I wiped it away. Windows watch—

Sarah Attayek

MY FIRST KISS, MY FIRST FUCK, MY FIRST CAR,
MY FIRST PLACE, MY FIRST BOSS, MY FIRST WIFE,
BUT THE ONLY THING I REMEMBER—IS YOU

BART VAN GOETHEM

Viscous secrets, sparkling champagne. Some things, once opened, cannot be closed. "Don't pry, little girl." Mama poured out another

N J Crosskey

When momma left, all 6 of us cried vinegar tears
Back East, had milk and honey. We had thirsty dirt
Her dust hadn't settled before the sky broke. We danced

Foy S. Iver

SHADE OF FORMER PALES
AGAINST REBIRTH OF SELF
NUMEROUS YET SAME

TRICIA DE JESUS

Passion etched beneath hunger
Claws outward
Scratched hues hide the words that speak

Bill A.

Castaways—we clung to the shape
Of a hollow band. Sallow and waning,
We could merely pencil in the depth of us

Elaine Marie McKay

She scrubs the outside disguising the inside
Ignoring beatings from the silent sun
Leaving everything watered down

Elisa Parker

Eyes closed, warmth expands in contained explosions,
Filling my body with the essence of lives unknown;
Time capsules revealed like a core of peat

A.J. Walker

THE NIGHT CRACKED OPEN
AND TOMORROW BLED SLOWLY
THROUGH OUR FINGERS

JACKI DONNELLAN

THE SPECKLED CLOTH OF THE FIRMAMENT
HANGS MAJESTICALLY O'ER THE DAY'S LIGHT
GAINING DOMINANCE. BECOMING. ESTABLISHING ITS RULE

MARK MORRIS

Casting out for ghost pots
Sunk on the waves, they say
It's like falling asleep in a shadow

DAZMB

> On the edge, ablaze!
> Why cling to reason
> This universe knows not of logic

David Shakes

One edges, tidies, snips, and trims
Who knows nothing
Of dreams and whims

                                        Marie Elena Good

Pale eyes gazing, the breeze tufts white, thinning hair
Feathered, frayed apron hem wilted across your thighs
Memories fractured, fading. Ah, but smell of pie and lilies

Jennifer Bakkerud

Mortality came to tea, Pointing out
All the clues beneath the flowery napkins
And peeling all the icing off the buns

Jacki Donnellan

Your screwed up words ball into a fist. Doubled over,
I squint at the seesaw world through bruised vision
And spit out letters like broken teeth

Elaine Marie McKay

Mourning-doved, I brood
Loss crissed across splendor
Where they say you soar

> Nancy Chenier

ZIPPED UP, BUTTONED DOWN, KNOT FAST,
AND YET THE BONES OF ME PROTRUDE
THROUGH EVERY RIP AND TEAR

JACKI DONNELLAN

Nature strung up and beaten like a slave
Welts appeared like dried riverbeds and speechless chimes
Winter came like a bandage too late

Brian Hollander

Windswept bones, a birdcage, where razor-winged
Blackbirds fly. Slashing my heart to ribbons, screeching
Songs so sorrowful, I dare not open my mouth—

Nan Holmes

Across millions of miles, light-years, and parsecs
Across hundreds of epochs, eras, and eons
The only life to ever exist, slowly annihilates itself

Carlos Orozco

Tonight, I hold a vigil for my heart
For galaxies overshot, for universes found and lost—
After, I'll sleep beneath brighter stars & dream of atlases

Ruth Long

DESICCATED, THIS WARP AND WEFT
WEAVES A SHROUD, A WINDING CLOTH
INTO A TAPESTRY OF WHAT ONCE HAD BEEN

STEPHANIE ELLIS

Lonely lost buoy bobbing through life
Waiting for some tired swimmer seeking surcease
Bored and hungry, I eat a seagull's cry

DeRicki Johnson

I SPY THROUGH THE KEYHOLE OF CANDY COLOURED GRAVES;
CHERRY KNOCK AT HEADSTONES
COLLECTING WHISPERS THROUGH THE GRAIN

ELAINE MARIE MCKAY

National Poetry Day
Theme 2015: Light

"If I had the words,
I wouldn't have taken so many photos."
~Matt Adamik

"If I had the photos,
I wouldn't have used so much ink…"
~Grace Black

Photo Credit Matt Adamik

Watching the last dregs of the sunset
Shimmering in the hope-stains
on the ground

Jacki Donnellan

When all the colors are a few shades darker
And the world is silent and indistinct
Hope is hidden, locked inside the lesser things

Carlos Orozco

An indeterminate messenger, it's either packet or wave
Or a luminous ghost of all the things we've seen
It's a memory bound in time, forever timeless

Mark Morris

I'm a drop in the ocean, unnoticed
You're a jewel on a leaf
Filling my whole world with sunlit fire

Tamara Shoemaker

You, converse to my inverse,
Matter to my antimatter, will they ever
See the nature of our symbiotic love?

Foy S. Iver

Cutting through darkness
Even a dew drop of hope
Will cast a shadow

Nan Holmes

Devouring the daylight,
Dainty dew drops adorn the dirt
With kisses of dawn

Sarah Attayek

"Lend to me your troubled ear,
Cry no more, now I'm here"
You said that, then disappeared—

Matt Milano

Beneath a waning moon
Love's eternal afterglow
Reveals halted dreams

Marie Elena Good

Veins intertwine, yet rays pass through
Never would have imagined, you so small
Could leave a shadow so huge

Lauren Akers Chiles

I am but a fly in amber
Seeker of Life's breadthless truths
Entombed in all Its answers

DeRicki Johnson

Slicing under the nighttime doorway, meant you were home
Piercing through morning dew drops, meant it was day
Blinking from tiny floating bodies, meant it was summer

Casey Rose Frank

Inside the circular pool of your mind
Is an overgrown jungle of thought
Reflecting its madness outward for all to see

Jennifer Todhunter

I kneel, before a change of season
Sun-fast orb…opposed I drift, on Autumn's wake
I time my sleep on veins of winter, rebel hibernation

Bev Flynn

The daybreak will not greet me this blithe morning
I bid a fondest farewell, two seasons ago. My illumination
Is of a different ilk now, wreathed in shrouded smiles

Tricia De Jesus

She cried and cried until the very sky took her,
And her crying fell as rain on the turning leaves
To be drunk, drop upon drop, by the cruel trees

David W. Blackstone

By the time I reach you
I will already be gone
Words are star fossils

Brian Hollander

Sky screams scarlet
Gloaming glints gone
Night nears now

Dave James Ashton

I try to grasp at colors—yet none can be found
As the air takes my breath, disappearing ever slowly
Morning's cold recurrence, daylight fading, slight return

Brian Puglisi

picked-over ideas, paradigms rusted and rooted
in Quinine blind minds with pinpricked light for brains,
their stark constellations tell the future like the past

Sherry Sutton Curtiss

Kindling tiny beacons—I illuminate your path to me,
A vigil of star shimmering sequins in the darkness. Waiting.
Praying you reach me before I burn away and out.

F.E. Clark

That lemon day, we heard butterfly wings whisper lavender
Words to the trees. Lids jammed tight; airplane arms;
Only sunbeams flying home in glass jars

Elaine Marie McKay

Subtle dew catching life, dancing
Gently rolling down the slope, falling
Life escaping in a quick splash, breaking

Mira Day

Hope drips from leaves of disparity
Falling into the gaping mouths of shattered souls
Clawing their way to an ethereal sunrise

Hannah Fields

Give me a little less each day, until
Things become as they are, and words disappear
Into weightless photons of infinite energy

DAZMB

"You can't fight the sunrise dear," she whispered,
painting a bright smile onto ashen canvas.
"Pull the drapes so no one can see the cobwebs."

N J Crosskey

As dawn slips through bedroom glass, a
Wedge of sun blooms on her pale left breast
A cozy trespasser on a blue autumn morning

Chris Milam

God sheds a final bitter tear upon his dying creation, inside
Its spherical perfection lie possibilities we've squandered
He says: "Let there be darkness" everywhere there is—

David Shakes

As a dry leaf cradles the morning dew
While the sleeping forest dreams of the sea
So shall I, cling to your smile

Karl A. Russell

Dumbstruck I stand, in awe and humility,
Celestial radiance streaming through foliage:
The silent voice of God

Geoff Holme

Star life, star strife, only star that dares tonight
I wish I may, I pray we might
Live to see another night

Michael Seese

Rays of sunshine wash over the early morning dew
Waking up every drop
Boiling them till they burst

Bart Van Goethem

Dawn breaks the horizon
Falls in a comfort dusk
Life is ablaze with…

Bill A.

Fierce, it pierces the page—
Plumbs rainy travails, scales jubilant summits,
Warms the skin of inky landscapes

Ruth Long

An indigo curtain shrouds the world's stage
Until night retires, when it rises on life
Admits the glimmer of a more hopeful day

Stephanie Ellis

You reach, swim, somersault: breaching the stillness,
But quietly. Dreaming, I hold you to my shoulder,
Speaking the name I don't yet know

Emily Livingstone

Bare trees stand like Zulu warriors along the ridge tops,
casting skeletal shadows across uncertain land. Burnished
leaves drift and scab disguising gateways to other realms—

A.J. Walker

You're a gem sunken into crude oil,
People, including me, only see the shining beauty,
Not realizing from whence you came

Brett Milam

Soft glow, a trinity
Of thought, of moments, of heat
An incandescent memory

Augusta Dorman

this watery world—
dew on a leaf,
spinning around the sun

Voima Oy

Autumn was the lifeline
holding the sun
a shining crystal ball

Christine Holden

Fragile structures, intersecting, create
Swift stories, flesh-formed. Overhead,
Infinity circles, her habitual shadow on bone within skin

Catherine Connolly

last kiss shivers: a droplet lingering on desiccation
best left parched
than tormented by the memory of moisture

Nancy Chenier

The Fall of it all
And trees soon turn toward decay
Here I sit, a pool of paged white-space

Grace Black

INDEX

WINNERS YEAR ONE 1

DAVID W. BLACKSTONE	35
DAVID BORROWDALE	14
NANCY CHENIER	12
LAUREN AKERS CHILES	19
CATHERINE CONNOLLY	45
SHERRY SUTTON CURTISS	32
MIRA DAY	15
DAZMB	39
JACKI DONNELLAN	43
STEPHANIE ELLIS	34
HANNAH FIELDS	31
CASEY ROSE FRANK	10, 16, 21, 38, 40
CHRISTINE HOLDEN	44
GEOFF HOLME	6
NAN HOLMES	4, 22, 37
FOY S. IVER	30, 36, 41
ROSE KETRING	17
MATT LASHLEY	11
EMILY LIVINGSTONE	28
ELAINE MARIE MCKAY	23, 24
CHRIS MILAM	2
BRETT MILAM	20
MATT MILANO	5
CARLOS OROZCO	25
VOIMA OY	26
KT PHILLIPS	9
BRIAN PUGLISI	13

IMAGE RONIN	3
KARL A. RUSSELL	8
MICHAEL SEESE	18, 27
DAVID SHAKES	7
TAMARA SHOEMAKER	29
JENNIFER TODHUNTER	42
PAUL JOHN WELSH	33

ARTISTS YEAR ONE 47

MATT ADAMIK	56-57
TRACY ANN	52-53
GIDGET BATES	48-49
BORIS BODEN	54-55
F. E. CLARK	58-59
BEV FLYNN	60-61
ADRIANA HAWKS	64-65
DAVID SHAKES	50-51
LISA SHAMBROOK	66-67
SOULHEARTS	68-69
KARIN TAYLOR	62-63

SPECIAL CHALLENGE YEAR ONE	71

BILL A.	87
DAVE JAMES ASHTON	77
SARAH ATTAYEK	82
JENNIFER BAKKERUD	96
DAVID BORROWDALE	72, 73
NANCY CHENIER	99
F. E. CLARK	80
N J CROSSKEY	84
DAZMB	93
TRICIA DE JESUS	86
JACKI DONNELLAN	81, 91, 97, 100
AUGUSTA DORMAN	76
STEPHANIE ELLIS	74, 105
BEV FLYNN	78
MARIE ELENA GOOD	95
BRIAN HOLLANDER	101
NAN HOLMES	102
FOY S. IVER	85
DERICKI JOHNSON	75, 106
EMILY LIVINGSTONE	79
RUTH LONG	104
ELAINE MARIE MCKAY	88, 98, 107
MARK MORRIS	92
CARLOS OROZCO	103
ELISA PARKER	89
DAVID SHAKES	94
BART VAN GOETHEM	83
A.J. WALKER	90

Light Prompt Poems 109

Acknowledgements

This collection has been a labor of love, a year-long endeavor, and it wouldn't have come to fruition without the immeasurable support of all that actively participate in the weekly challenges at Thee Line Thursday.

I am truly appreciative of the constant inspiration and camaraderie of many talented individuals I've met through the community of writers and artists that gather to contribute each week.

I wish each of you much continued success throughout your journeys; the well-worn path, the off-beaten trail, and each diversion in-between, there is poetry to be seen—

Love & Ink,
Grace Black

About The Contributors

Bill A.
　Therapy
　Release Escape
　My soul which bleeds

　@adaydreamwriter

Matt Adamik
　He is of the quiet moment keepers.
　Feeding on the cracks of light that highlight pieces of
　life. He devotes all of himself to this vocation.

　@MattAdamikPhoto
　facebook.com/MattAdamikPhotography

Tracy Ann
　Behind the lens of her camera, from across the pond
　She's a perfectly imperfect mother of one
　a kind hearted joker, loving and strong

　@Sapphire83
　facebook.com/Tracy.A.M.photography

Dave James Ashton
　Currently a chalkie but starting to write.
　A short piece, a silly piece, a long loquacious piece.
　Clattering keys help to find his peace.

　@davejamesashton

Sarah Attayek
One step at a time to run farther.
One word at a time to write longer.
One breath at a time to breathe deeper.

@RTayaket

Jennifer Bakkerud
Extroverted introvert who cocoons daily with her cat, a pen in one hand...a lint brush in the other, Seeking that elusive word which will make the sentence sing—

@JennyBakkerud

Gidget Bates
The heart takes the shots
Tears and smiles this side of a frame
Her soul owns the camera no matter what

@gidgetbates
gidgetbates.com

Grace Black
Black mingles with words
As she navigates this realm
Poetry & Flash like her coffee—dark

@blackinkpinkdsk
graceblackwrites.com
threelinethursday.com

DAVID W. BLACKSTONE
He's a musician, composer, & writer from Gaithersburg, Maryland. Has played trombone professionally, even though he knows better. Currently a leaf on the wind.

@DavidWriting
agincourtdb.com

BORIS BODEN
"Somewhere Between A Flower And A Chainsaw." He's a full-time cynic with hopes of someday becoming a skeptic. Also know as the 'Secret Weapon'

woodyradio.com
@Borisasaurus

DAVID BORROWDALE
Science editor by day
Flash fiction writer
the rest of the time

@MicroBookends
microbookends.com

NANCY CHENIER
Coiling an identity in three iterations,
She'll inevitably shed self
somewhere in the spaces.

@rowdy_phantom

Lauren Akers Chiles
Spanish teacher by day, writer by night, wife always. A lover of God, books, music, people, short & sweet. Resident of the Midwest with dreams of distant lands.

@howdylauren
howdylauren.wordpress.com

F. E. Clark
Based in NE Scotland, she takes inspiration from the magical: mountains, sea, sky & woodlands around her. Artist, writer, crane-folder, hat-wearer, & Flashdog.

@feclarkart
feclarkart.com

Catherine Connolly
Word worlds
Transcribed
Into independence

@FallIntoFiction
fallintofiction.blogspot.co.uk

N J Crosskey
She is a mother, writer, and night worker. Crosskey hopes one day to be a novelist. Until then, she'll rely on caffeine for her state of consciousness.

@NJCrosskey
njcrosskey.wordpress.com

SHERRY SUTTON CURTISS
As a mother of two daughters and speech language pathologist, writing is a perfect forum for Sherry not to lose touch with living in the moment

@RealSherryLS

MIRA DAY
New Adult Romance Writer with a Passion for food.
Southern Girl through and through
Exclamation points are my favorite!

@MiraDayAuthor
MiraMichelleDay.com

dAZMB
husband—loving
father—doting
personally—vibrating with the terror of existence

@dAZMB

TRICIA DE JESUS
Lover of thought provocation, helpless, furry creatures, and the exquisite pursuit of the unknown.

@PhynneBelle

JACKI DONNELLAN
    Living in the centre of the map
    A mother in her equinox years
    enjoying the view

    @DonnellanJacki

AUGUSTA DORMAN
    Tempest in a well mannered jar
    Word riddled sometimes world worn
    Always a glass half full

    @tinydrifter

STEPHANIE ELLIS
    Pen in hand, her mind drifts beyond to shadow lands
    Unleashing dark-winged stories and unrhymed lines
    On a speculative world.

    @el_stevie
    stephellis.weebly.com

HANNAH FIELDS
    Author of "Dreams and Revelations"
    Wanderer, poet, coffee addict,
    dog lover, and raving music enthusiast.

    @Oh_Panorama
    thepanoramicdynamic.com

Bev Flynn

She's a reticent poet, who casts words beside riverbanks. A summer soul…that basks, in shadow Found meandering on Twitter and Instagram

@BevFlynn0331
instagram.com/bevflynn0331/

Casey Rose Frank

Traded cities for hometown greenery. Seeking adventure, imaginary and real, great and small. Creating unlimited worlds with limited words.

@CaseyRoseFrank
caseyrosefrank.com

Marie Elena Good

Marie Elena is a recreational poet, relentless loser of words, loyal lover of children's stories, and fan of poem as a verb, and smile as a wardrobe.

picturedwords.me

Adriana Hawks

A Texas native & full-time IT Specialist with a passion for mixed-media art. Inspired by beauty found in the mysteries of nature and the mundane of ordinary life.

@chatagrl
instagram.com/chatagrl/

CHRISTINE HOLDEN
>Music is the food of all that I love
>A dreamer, a schemer, coffee drinker, cheese eater
>Playing on words, hoping to be heard.
>
>@chris_holden1

BRIAN HOLLANDER
>By the time I reach you
>I will already be gone
>Words are star fossils

GEOFF HOLME
>Reading—always slowly: absorb every word
>Writing—mostly briefly: cherish the #FlashDogs
>Arithmetic—not my forte: Three Lines are cool!
>
>@GeoffHolme

NAN HOLMES
>Fancied myself a painter till my paint ran dry
>Picked up a pen, through three little lines
>And found my voice again—
>
>@nholmes413

Foy S. Iver
Breaking my bones to find
The marrow of meaning
And feast

@fs_iver
foyiver.com

DeRicki Johnson
Aspiring writer and seeker,
wandering this mortal coil—Squirrel!
Also, dealing with 'focus' issues...

@derickijohnson
derickijohnson.wordpress.com

Rose Ketring
A practicing bibliophile who seeks refuge among dusty paper magic & the Dewey Decimal System. An inspiration pack-rat always looking for her next 'information high'

@blurosemd

Matt Lashley
Matt has a small hole in his frontal lobe where his creative juices randomly spill out—over speed bumps. Occasionally he enjoys sharing the splatters.

@MattLashley_

EMILY LIVINGSTONE
    With steadfast husband & curious dog, preparing for change, teaching & writing in New England, within reach of family, loving both quiet moments & music.

    @Emi_Livingstone
    emilylivingstone.wordpress.com

RUTH LONG
    Golden State native
    Reader, writer, and giggler
    Zealous believer in creative community

    @bullishink
    bullishink.com

ELAINE MARIE MCKAY
    She lives in Scotland with her husband, and often finds herself having to pretend to their four, young kids that she's not afraid of the dark.

    @Elaine173Marie

BRETT MILAM
    Bleeding ink and coffee on the
    white screen from Ohio; a student,
    and dog-lover, trying to outrun the shadows.

    @brett_milam
    brettmilam.com

CHRIS MILAM
A connoisseur of cheap cigarettes, too-sweet coffee, and morbid laziness. On most days he can be found sulking arrogantly from his perch on the couch.

@blukris
wispofsmokemilam.wordpress.com

MATT MILANO
Writing from the truth I see,
The easy ending's not for me.
Greetings friend, the name's Hati

@Cemodano

MARK MORRIS
A red-headed man from the land of the Queen,
A jack of all trades—many talents unseen—
Instills fire and passion into every scene.

CARLOS OROZCO
T-minus 10 until blastoff
The rockets are roaring
But I'm still not ready to leave

@goldzco21

VOIMA OY
She lives in Chicago near the expressway and the Blue Line trains. Her writing can be found in both FlashDog anthologies and online.

@voimaoy
welcometoveridian.wordpress.com

ELISA PARKER
Elisa Parker loves to write, especially poetry and narrative non-fiction. She has a B.A. in English. Elisa also loves to travel, sing, play the guitar and violin.

KT PHILLIPS
Born, raised and still resides in Southeast Louisiana. She's an avid reader, enjoys record collecting, the outdoors, and spending time with her family.

ktphillipswrites.wordpress.com

BRIAN PUGLISI
Sometimes he looks at something & can write quickly
Sometimes he looks forever and can write slowly
Sometimes the pictures fade and dreams take the lead

@brianpuglisi

IMAGE RONIN
   Writer of flash fiction
   And bad poetry
   Drinker of black coffee

   @ImageRonin

KARL A. RUSSELL
   A stew of dreams, desires, frailties and fears,
   Wrapped in the shape of a man, Let loose into the
   world through ink stained fingertips.

   @Karl_A_Russell

MICHAEL SEESE
   Michael Seese writes novels,
   short stories, flash fiction, plays, poetry,
   music, and the future.

   @MSeeseTweets
   MichaelSeese.com

DAVID SHAKES
   dabbles in painting with words & photographing small
   paragraphs. Enjoys the intensity of flash & poetry of
   TLT. Least hardworking of the Flashdogs, but he tries.

   @TheShakes72
   flickr.com/photos/theshakes72/

LISA SHAMBROOK
  Lisa loves weaving intricate stories inside her imagination. She's a writer, artist, photographer, and inspirational dreamer—and she adores dragons.

  @LisaShambrook
  lisashambrook.com

TAMARA SHOEMAKER
  Tamara has written ten novels and is adding more. She's a Flashdog, poet, wife, mom, all four. Friend of coffee and enemy of sleep. Hear her roar.

  @TamaraShoemaker

SOULHEARTS
  Life is fleeting, so she traps moments in photographs and words. Loving life and giving thanks while she still can. After all, we're just memories in the end.

  @soulhearts
  instagram.com/soulhearts

KARIN TAYLOR
  She looks at the world through as many different lenses of perspective and understanding as possible; She does this through a macro lens on her iPhone.

  @Karintaylor
  karintaylorphotography.tumblr.com

JENNIFER TODHUNTER
Jennifer is a number nerd by day, word fiddler at night. She enjoys dark, salty chocolate & running top speed in the other direction.

@JenTod_
foxbane.ca

BART VAN GOETHEM
Father. Copywriter. Drummer.
Facetious if necessary.
Insists he is not a poet.

@bartvangoetham

A.J. WALKER
Red man with Poised Pen and delusions of dark hair,
a user of words and diesel
and occasional eclectic use of grammar.

@zevonesque
zevonesque.com

PAUL JOHN WELSH
born in 1965, Glasgow, Scotland, Graduate of University of Glasgow, he'll write about anything because he wants to and always seems to have to.

@pauljohnwelsh
paulwelsh27.wordpress.com

About Three Line Thursday

The idea for Three Line Thursday was born from Grace Black's love of brevity. In a disposable, throwaway world our ever decreasing attention spans still seek moments of inspiration, and poetry has always been an effective way of conveying emotive resonance.

The creative world can be lonely and filled with rejection, and as a writer or artist sometimes we need to remind ourselves to get involved. Come up for air, loose ourselves from our pessimistic pits, and break free from our creative caves for a while.

Three Line Thursday is the spot to do just that: a place for inspiration and camaraderie, a place to encourage one another each week, a place to hone your craft—

Bringing people in the artistic community together, Three Line Poetry is beneficial on many levels. Learning how to say more with less is a useful tool for any writer. A visceral experience, whether you're a novice poet, writer, blogger, photographer, artist, or a seasoned professional, Grace believes everyone has something to contribute.

All are welcome! Come lay down ink...

threelinethursday.com

WE CUP OUR ACHE IN HANDS
DRAG OUR FEET ALONG WORN BOARDS TILL THE END
WHERE THE SOLSTICE OF OUR EVES ENGAGE IN INK

GRACE BLACK

Printed in Great Britain
by Amazon.co.uk, Ltd.,
Marston Gate.